"It is no accident that this confident, gorgeous book begins with and returns to the space probe Voyager I, still sending back its continuous data, despite everything. On his various journeys as a father, friend, reader, husband, citizen, Winger sends his data back, but this book is not a one-way transmission: with typical implicit grace and generosity, Winger thinks of us, on our journeys too. As he says to Voyager, and therefore to us, 'I want you to know, sailor, that all of us are with you.' These poems continually move with authentic surprise, wry intelligence, and humour, out of the ordinary, and into genuine communion. You can feel the generous attention to a reader, and presence of a companion, beaming you messages you didn't know you needed, but do."
— Matthew Zapruder, author of *Father's Day* and *Why Poetry*

"Wise, worrying, and playful, Winger's *It Doesn't Matter What We Meant* meditates on time, hope, complicity, and conscience; in short, on what it's like to be alive right now. No matter what we intended the future to look like ('Fifteen years ago, we'll colonize the moon'), this moment, for better and worse, is what we've made."
— Gil Adamson, author of *Ridgerunner*

"How do we see? What do we know? Curious and unsatisfied, Rob Winger's new collection *It Doesn't Matter What We Meant* seems to hang in the interval between approach and grasp. A speed trap, a birch tree, comets, neighbourhood restaurants, wind turbines, predictions for the future: all and more are scrutinized in the imaginative, questioning lines of these restless, conversational poems, where observation is both steadied by a level eye and lifted with a lyric buoyancy."
— David O'Meara, author of *A Pretty Sight*

"Shot through with the gorgeous possibilities of an often-impossible present, *It Doesn't Matter What We Meant* offers watchful snapshots of both galactic change and pocket change. In the driveway under the incandescent otherworld of space, urgent questions of access, agency, and inheritance thrum on every page. This is a collection that keeps the counsel of many seekers. Read it, and you'll be in excellent company."
— Erin Wunker, author of *Notes from a Feminist Killjoy*

ALSO BY ROB WINGER

Muybridge's Horse (2007)
The Chimney Stone (2010)
Old Hat (2014)

IT DOESN'T MATTER WHAT WE MEANT

poems

ROB WINGER

McClelland & Stewart

McClelland & Stewart and colophon are registered trademarks of Penguin Random House
Canada Limited.

Grateful acknowledgement is made to reprint the following previously published material:
Excerpt from *Selected Poems: The Vision Tree* by Phyllis Webb, © 1982, Phyllis Webb,
Talonbooks, Vancouver. Every effort has been made to trace copyright holders and to
obtain their permission for the use of copyright material. The publisher apologizes for
any errors or omissions and would be grateful if notified of any corrections that should be
incorporated in future reprints or editions of this book.

Published simultaneously in the United States of America.

Library and Archives Canada Cataloguing in Publication data is available upon request.

ISBN: 978-0-7710-2539-6
ebook ISBN: 978-0-7710-2540-2

Book design by Emma Dolan
Cover art: (pick up truck) Winslow Productions / Getty Images; (stars) Tiradae Manyum /
EyeEm / Getty Images; (satellite) NASA on the Commons / flickr
Typeset in Garamond by M&S, Toronto

Printed and bound in Canada

McClelland & Stewart,
a division of Penguin Random House Canada Limited,
a Penguin Random House Company
www.penguinrandomhouse.ca

1 2 3 4 5   25 24 23 22 21

Penguin
Random House
McCLELLAND & STEWART

CONTENTS

For
K.

1

STILL STILL

When I talk, again, about Voyager 1
out there beyond the heliosphere,
what I really mean is that
none of us recalls the birth canal.

And when I show you this photo
of my favourite painting, made in Paris
with palette knives in 1954, I'm giving you
my boyhood's village springs.

Every novelist's demilitarized zone
wants a good coconut beach.

The robins eating winter sumac mean
the oceans are deeper than we think.

So when I tell you the ladder's too short
to clean out the eavestroughs,
what I'm really saying is that
the ladder's too damned short
to clean out the stupid eavestroughs.

What I'm really saying is that bankers
still scavenge everybody's breadcrumbs.

The baseball at the height of its arc
in the outfield by the ears
of corn is every lost October leaf pile.

The bookmarks strewn across
our desktops mean we've forgotten
our grandmothers' birthdays;

and our once-read grad-school
textbooks will never be
the last ship out of Saigon.

Let's re-focus our blue-box cylinders;
there are still, right here, green points
in our gardens, pushing up
against three inches of April ice.

The chorus in your favourite song
is next year's coiled calendar.

So, when I tell you, again,
about Voyager 1 shutting down
its systems, measuring
interstellar gamma rays,
what I really mean is that
none of our kids
can ever be shielded
from even a single solar flare.

We tried to hold fast, but we were asleep.
Our holding was a dream about holding.
Or dreaming was our buried cargo hold.
We're shepherds, we said, without any sheep.
We offered our seeds and they were carried.
Who wants to be the ivy trained on brick?
Who needs to need to see beyond this creek?
At the shore, each wave could signal theory
but we focus, instead, on shade and breeze,
on picnic-basket fathers gone snow-blind.
Back inland, patriots carve centuries
out of California Joshua trees.
Heft, maybe. Sap. Desert glue. Tundra rind.
Hold fast, we tell those dreams; we're still at sea.

Since there are still turtle bridges;
since battlefronts end up ditches;
since sugar cane.

Since the online castle walls glitch out;
since highway shoulders crumble into seeds;
since seed bombs come lupine, come daffodil.

At the cashier, we won't cheer for blue beards;
the sea arrives at our coastal mouth organs;
the earrings pool inside our ears, still gold.

Since this placard is no brick wall;
since the glove compartment bump stocks
come with manuals, come heat.

Since middle-class parents used to be ash;
since your sheets had no thread count;
since spreadsheets can't record handholding.

In the foothill forest, mountain ranges are fairy tales;
winter whiteout, summer blisters;
your first cracked window, your first No.

Even the North Pacific garbage-island death zone;
even the microplastics in a fresh trout gut;
even the carefully stacked receipts.

Even the gale-force crumpled siding;
even the springs turned sulphur;
even marching one-way streets.

Since used batteries;
since the recycling plant sorting accidental compost;
since the unread books on sagging shelves.

Even if you try to count paintings for red ink;
even if the hillside is just a hillside;
even if the fields are fields.

Even the old lecterns, falling;
even the tired acetate come missile;
even if maps redrawn, settled, emptied.

Since the humanitarian gala's stale champagne;
since this kid putting the dollar-store toy back;
since the factory floor's punch clock, its severed digits.

In those years, people will say, we lost track of the meaning of we.
In those years, velvet barbarism.
In those years, arterial plaque still fixed.

In those years, post-committee craft ales.
In those years, pile-on retweet retro-gangs.
In those years, pro/con, neo-/post-, anti-/trust.

But we don't live in a perfect world;
even the goldfinch sunset;
even the summer meadow.

THE WHITE APRON

I'm easing this engine between
painted lines and meters. It's morning.
On the radio: more bad news.

This neighbourhood's worn out
but used to be brand new sedans,
fresh window dressings, the polished
marble hopes of heavy manufacturing.
Someone has tenderly placed red
mulch beneath all the sidewalk saplings.

Some whipping down this one-way street
are fresh from the lot. Others, ringed
in rust, push odometer century marks,
cheat E-tests, use rags for gas caps.
Around the corner is a pre-packed library,
an empty gallery, parks littered
with rye bottles, glistening metal slides.
Every golden age is a close-up city creek.

Inside *The White Apron*, newly reclaimed
barn boards dignify the tables.
Red seat cushions gleam.
The open kitchen means
anyone can watch the cooks.

The server brings a bowl
of creamers, a plate loaded
with 7am carbohydrates,
a giant silver carafe.
Her shift must just have started.
She hasn't yet been heckled, hasn't yet
returned men to their downtown
concrete dreams.

I'm typing now, fitting the keyboard in
beside these plated potatoes,
building this capsule for you.

I'm trying to detail what happened here
and how it felt. I'm wondering whether
or not humans are vile time bombs.
I'm trying to believe in childhood
hair ribbons, in mourning doves.

I want us to consider, despite new plaster
or shining click-laminate floorboards,
how any building can ever know its place,
if place is only I-beams,
if place is just a feeling.

On the other side of the window,
the bus station is swollen
in old departures.
The barred storefronts
all used to be owned
by someone else.

Let's finish our eggs.
Let's tip generously.
Almost no one else is out of bed.
Things are about to happen.

We'll unlock the doors remotely.
Will turn our engines over
and pull into the nearest lanes.

Remember: all the radio signals
we've ever heard are still out there.
If we could accrue enough speed,
we'd catch them less than halfway to Polaris.

Out there, with carefully calibrated
cruise control, each of us
only bits of light, we could rest,
I think, if we wanted, in any single era's hit
parade, finally finding our golden tickets
to the factory's last shipping bay.

When all the wind turbines turn
away from sun,

we'll put our faith in a tiny spectrum of waves
from California's widest field array.

So much of what matters
is conditional.

Hey, Hydro line. I get you.
This rubber wrench might ground us.

Picture a picture of yourself at ten, maybe.
Is the light on the paper still moving?

When all the Pacific's plastic islands
finally measure reef bleach,

we'll put these photographs in leather albums
to defend the analog comeback of vinyl, again.

Maybe that's too much.
There are still sunsets, after all.

Seeing Venus sit there, early evening,
means we're ready for robins.

Every pet we've got we'll lose;
and our phones will never smell like paper.

Even if all the bears move in to bungalows
the riverbed rocks will still be smooth.

Hey, Mercury. I see you.
Let's agree to disagree.

RED BED

"Tall, plump, brilliantly red and rich in both color and flavor!
Bake, boil, or simmer; they are quite versatile.
Excellent yields leave plenty for processing."
  —*Thompson & Morgan*, Quality English Seeds since 1855

We'd like to claim all hurt goes country,
that every fieldstone marker crumbles every March.

But out on the salt marsh, that's just veneer.
Way back when, Maine gardeners were serious:

they named their seeds for the virile Volga
or Wu emperor's fever,

a Song cure for plague
or Ming general's suicide tea,

Queen Victoria's opium
after Marco Polo's apothecary;

Ornamental, European Wild, Garden, Bastard;
Sweet Round-Leaved Duck, Wine Plant;

Himalayan, Sikkim, Chinese, East Indian,
English, Tartarian, Chipman's Canada Red.

Is every stalk a summit?

No matter. Your grave will grow
its crustose lichens anyhow,

gold cobblestone or map, all mesic
births and fallen arms,

your Malachi windows clouded blue
so long as the ice age lasts.

In the next century, houses will be furnished in steel
and computers will weigh only a ton and a half.
Fifteen years ago, we'll colonize the moon,
and last year, our under-sea bathyscaphe cities
will be the pride of frogmen
at the stellar world's fair.

Flying saucers will shame the Golden Gate Bridge
as we zip to work in jetpacks under biodomes,
each home portably self-sustainable,
with every Cyclops human gazing out its single eye
where the bridge of its nose used to be.
Square tomatoes, for perfect sandwiches,

will be served with spousal "grouch pills"
before TV sets with olfactory remotes.
Democracy, dead by 1950, and the internet fad over
by '96, wireless technology will prove war
and high-speed trains ridiculously impossible
—people can't breathe at such velocity.

Behemoth human women, six feet tall,
will never be prime minister in my lifetime, but still
at home with nuclear-powered vacuum cleaners,
which will be everywhere in a decade,
as common as these in-class electrocution machines
that help us all to spell without the letter Q.

The horse is here to stay, but your mail
will arrive daily, New York to Australia
in hours, via guided missiles.
Apple will never make a cell phone, and steaks
will cost a buck, delivered by kangaroo butlers
and simian chauffeurs. We might as well get used to it.

SPEED TRAP

We all know they set up under overpasses,
after cloverleafs, against water barrels
clustered under light standards,
but out on the highway,
we're still strangers, each cabin
an atlas charting concrete.

Inside the trap, discussions
—of the new president or
polar vortex or that late-quarter
record-breaking comeback
that ultimately falls short—
are arrested.

We depress our own pedals,
observe our instruments
reading retrograde red
in the rear-view mirror,
both hands properly positioned
on the wheel.

Outside radar, velocity is less a rule
than a feeling. Nobody obeys
their own speedometers.
The freeway's a flight path for
red-tailed hawks, we might say,
a funeral for blazingly exiled foxes.

So we aim for fresh flowerbeds,
well-stocked garages, the bark-filled
lanes where we kill our engines.
Tonight, covered in our own crisp sheets,
will we dream of speed guns, or, haltingly,
the open exits for everything they bracket?

The speed of light is no hummingbird,
so can that nectar-filled bell hanging
from the blue spruce out front
ever affirm the Cosmic Microwave Background?

All of us are moving. A thousand miles
each circular hour, slung
in equatorial hammocks, says Google,
but less at the poles, less in Canada.

It says this in its little robot voice,
as though attempting to remain impartial.
We're going through all this darkness, it says,
at 30 kilometres a second; that's 67,000 miles an hour.

And our whole system, the voice says, zips around
some Galactic Centre at another 220 clicks
a second, another 490,000 miles an hour.
Light years make no sense. They're Rilke's angels.

The bread rises in the window's radiation.
The gurgling pond or winter ice crystals
or sleepy nuclear warheads all drift,
as Hawking's Perfect Paul might tell us,

towards some essential prom date
—lensing standard candle supernovas,
pummelled by extragalactic cosmic rays—
that experts call, expertly, "The Great Attractor,"

a theory of mass out there, six trillion miles from here.
You had me at Milky Way, I want to say to Neil deGrasse Tyson.
You had me when we located our own little sphere
in celestial arms, in dark energy nobody remotely understands.

Lit by pulsars, denying lambda, neutrinos everywhere,
my legs carry me to the nightfall window. Its old light
is only now arriving from some other understanding.
The tracks in the snow tell me something small was in the yard,

but left. Voyager 1, I'm thinking of you out there,
past the heliopause. Last month, they turned on
your backup thrusters for the first time in 37 years.
And they worked. But you're still unplugged.

You haven't posted a picture in years.
I want your gentle dish to feel loved.
I want the duty of your pictograms expunged.
I want you to know, sailor, that all of us are with you.

ESCARPMENT

i.

We've come here, cliffside, to admire
this steel assemblage poised against
tankers sluicing past the Western wharf.
And we've come without irony:
those flames, we say, that's beauty.
From here, every shoreline forge is automatic.

We've parked our parents' sedans
at the escarpment edge
overlooking a distant harbour's ink.
These flames we read as clean, as possible.
The shore tells us how to build each tower,
each incinerator, how to manage each steel

stair circumambulating the blast furnace,
the way the lake stays still, streetlights
trimming our easy views of Ursa Major.
This is before the sun got stuck,
with now-felled emerald ashes,
pocket waterfalls, concrete, all of it

beyond out-of-sight crack houses
later bulldozed, past the now-closed
downtown mall, the neglected, first-class gallery,
the industrial circuit board that held up
the edge of a fiery, iced-up lake.
From here, these flames, apartment-buildings high,

seemed brightest. We watched them
oxidize into Irish castle moss rot,
nineteenth-century bricks eroding
into heritage pockmarks, into chickenpox
scar pits. From here, there's only light.
From here: coke, slag, ballast.

ii.

My basement is dirt-packed, is limestone crumble.
My basement is damp and dark, the chain swaying
from its single bulb, impossible to locate.
My basement stairs lined with fishing gear
fixed to walls painted sky blue.
My basement crawlspace. My basement lit,
finally, by that bulb, to reveal, abandoned
on the packed earth, snakeskins and trapped mice,
broken rotors, the furnace a hulking
hidden family secret, its oil drum outside,
distant, behind the shed where we pee
when the bathroom's occupied,
where the pipes terminate in septic beds,
where we bury family pets with crosses,
where none of the trees were planted,
but grew their own roots, before us.
The basement window caked with dirt.
The basement past the winter pantry,
packed with bottled potatoes and pears.
The basement stairs down to skin and chain
and earth and limestone crumble.

iii.

Those of us who grew up here livestream
the demolition of the Nanticoke coal plant,
the one looming over that ball diamond perched
so close to the edge of Erie, where so many fathers
spent their muscles moving carbon into water.

Here, we watched ships navigate the piers,
watched lines emerge in crisp logic
from the belly of generational machinery,
watched women try to enter all that certitude,
mocked for overalls, for helmets or steel-toed surety.

Those coal pyramids, we thought, were filled with promise.
That pitch clutch meant family business,
meant our picnic baskets could be stuffed.
The lake's still gorgeous, we'd say. The water
keeps going. Don't worry. The Lord, some of us

said, back then, will provide; the world
is wider than we think.

iv.

Passing this inlet's
neighbouring nuclear plant,
I'm twenty-eight years late for
An Atlas of the Difficult World,
but its coordinates still grid
every present survey.

This lake that separates
me from a Rich America
is molten silver, yet cool,
swallowing its own horizon
so cloud and earth become water,
turn silk. What can it mean to worry

for each woman on the platform
opposite this window?

What can we mean when
each present-tense stays still,
when the flowers you planted,
watered, cut, collected in this vase,
refuse to dry out, remain
terribly fragrant on our kitchen table?

The breakwaters out the window
surrounded by difficult swells
are artificially powerful.
What can it mean to see them
anticipating future surges?
How might summer remember ice

without becoming dependent
on worry, without seeing

each of these twenty-eight years
as a late spring that doesn't bud?
I don't want to assassinate
the men who insist, the boys
ignoring caged kids
at the border, then or now.

But *these are the materials.*
This is the shape of the inlet,

gloriously green, filled with fish,
perched against the failing,
cracked reactor that depends on it.
You knew, you say,
that I would be *reading this poem,*
listening for something, torn

between bitterness
and hope.

The power plant and the inlet,
the will to change and change,
the great lake's tiny tidal pull
and faint connections to the lost,
crashing, far Atlantic. Is this shore
the something I'm supposed to hear?

Maybe there's no such thing as transparent
glass. Maybe you're teaching us that every
window is a prescription lens, that each
horizon is always a past or future accidental.
I'm leaning in now, listening.
Rust collides with the train's wheels

somewhere deep below us, tracks
leading to the line's set terminus.

v.

I've still got no model for Three Mile Island,
no Fukushima Daiichi, no family
album from Hiroshima.

And by now, we've all heard about the lost wolves
returning to Chernobyl, how they and their quarry
now outnumber their non-mutant Red Forest

counterpart packs, seven to one. Our exclusion-zone drones
find rooftop white-tailed eaglets, Przewalski's horses nuzzling
convenience store shelves, scientists still declaring

danger at the epicentre: uninhabitable, they say,
for the next twenty thousand years. But here,
in lockdown, fake Venetian dolphins or Asian murder wasps

notwithstanding, each false occupant is evicted. So: this
whale shark in Guanabara Bay, that rare Spanish brown bear,
these wild Kashmiri mountain goats filling the Welsh streets,

red fox pups on closed Toronto boardwalks,
Santiago pumas, Lopburi turf-war macaques,
genteel English antlers, cracker-crunching sika deer in Nara;

these Indian wild boars and their mangy mutt antagonists
or these lions hugging hot South African asphalt, wild dogs
on an eighteenth green, a coyote passing City Lights bookstore.

Back home, we look up at all the new galaxies
unmapped in our childhoods, pinpoints
just captured by our latest machines;

that none of us can imagine
the end of the sentence means
none of us can punctuate our predicates.

vi.

At twelve, I make a fine cast
from the short dock to pull this hooked pickerel
from Honey Harbour, its razored snout.

How many creatures had I already killed by then?
Bullfrogs and crayfish by the dozen,
squadrons of wasps, ants, a milk snake.

But this body ripped clean from its element,
thrashing on the swallowed hook,
shows me a first eye, a primary translation.

It dies there on the line,
the side of its body curving,
its gills slick and desperate.

Later, my grandfather helps me select
the surest stone and hands me the knife.
I gut and clean, cut loose its sides,

return the skeleton and head and fins
to the water, wonder over blood
and organs, over the heat in them.

vii.

Blue-bin duty, petition form letter,
posts and posts and posts
delineate our private acreage.

That I see Kilimanjaro losing its snow
doesn't mean I see the sky
or its histories, the sea.

At the Flaggy Shore, following Seamus,
I find almost no plastic, almost only
Burren rock and wind,

a farmer mending his electric fence,
a single cow out there at the point
with its Martello tower.

But all of us drive here; all of us park.
Not a single animal fashions rags.
Not a single swan needs a garbage can.

Later, at the airport, security agents remove,
wrapped in my hidden long johns, my carefully
selected stones and place them,

rescued, in a moulded tray, their perfect
rings left there, heritage items,
possible weapons, gone.

I think of those stones, now,
here at my basement desk.
I wonder if they'll ever see another sea.

2

ALL BOAT

LETTER TO IRON HEINRICH

I hid in the lime spring, see,
until the sun filled up with her.

I knew her golden ball would fall. *Love me*,
I said, when it did. She knew what I meant.

I had short little legs, then. I couldn't keep up.
It took me a day to get to her gilded table.

But the father and I had an understanding.
A promise is a promise, he said.

He's the one who ordered us to the bedroom
where she hurled me, warts and all, against that wall.

But we showed her, didn't we, Heinrich?
I shed my frogskin right between her silken sheets.

Does every princess only want to turn us
into silkworm pantaloons?

I'm writing, now, to ask for the broken iron
that fell from your heart that morning.

We need rings, Heinrich. And we'll want you
on the carriage. We've still got loads of work to do.

after "The Frog King, or Iron Heinrich"

Out in this valley, we've sprayed for weeds;
that's why we came here.

Sometimes a single honeybee
navigates the wilting marigolds,
mirroring the sun's arc
over glacial rivers.

Here's what we depend on—
Motown LP collections, movies
on white comic heroes, bagels
sold in the Plateau, or Virginia
Woolf novels, included last-minute
on the syllabus, the last Lego brick
that builds the tower tall for prisons.

Coming to this valley, we wanted
to confirm our capital,
to suture these coal towns
with silent, silver prints

that look like here, but were imported
wholesale from the city, purchased
with salaries we think we've earned—
nothing need be erased, we think,
everything is gorgeous in ruins.

Out here, helplessness is no choice, is it?

We're helpless, we say, against the mountain
stream's pull, for instance. We won't let you
speak about drowning, only rescue,
when good, true men step from banks
to lacerate emergencies.

The early ice will come again this fall
so Cassiopeia will match our currents,
both reflected in our spotless corneas
as though everyone sees the same pictures
when they stride away from water,

as though each fisher holds the same rod,
as if the winter roads weren't already closed
to all but local traffic.

after "Trying to Talk with a Man"

LETTER TO A GRANDDAUGHTER

In the woods, all men are wolves.
Pins and Needles, hot bread and milk.

They bottle blood and cube muscles,
open our mouths to pour them in.

The cat calls every one of us a "slut."
The beds tell us to strip,

but slowly, our layers burning,
each inch covered in upright hair.

That she pisses outside, a thread
on her ankle, is the fairy magic, here.

The fact he can't catch up is just
dumbed-down happy-ever-after.

after "The Story of Grandmother"

RED TRUCK TREATY

i.

These roads were named for the red
country trucks we were given as boys,
stick shifts polished by our fathers,
uncles, grandfathers, good men
all, each a tiny killer.
We call the land a mirror,
then gather the ants in the doorway
into tidy paper towels,
folding to hide the way
their little bodies break.
Those damned things, we think,
they're such a fucking nuisance.

ii.

We steer our trucks down rural routes,
swearing at the women picking apples.
We mumble something about their hips, maybe,
about the goddamn government's wussy
tax policies. We drive off leaving dust plumes
that cover them in fine, invisible sand.

iii.

In the city, there's just too much.
You have to walk right past
the dirty street dudes—
who knows what they'd do?
There's garbage everywhere.
There are so many fucking cars.
There's a stray German shepherd down
every alley. We'd rather the pine trees,
rather stack cords of winter wood
knowing exactly which piece goes where.

iv.

We thought, by now, we'd have cottages
and Cadillacs, like our grandfathers did,
like our fathers, too, some of them.
I think about those women on that road.
I think about their fine, sandy fingers.
I think about the lake where I'd build the best
deck ever, the foot-long bass I'd pull from the water.
I think about how easy it might be to turn the wheel.

v.

I didn't want to have to teach you all this.
It's not easy. Those statues by my pond
I inherited from my grandmother.
They're just men holding lanterns,
fishing. They're part of history is all.
Why can't you leave well enough the fuck alone?

vi.

I'm not political, but we built this place.
And I work for a living.
See these hands? They're not like yours.
Not everyone expects a handout.
See my daughter, here, in her crib,
up at night—I share the feedings—she
deserves a better future, doesn't she?
No kid of mine should have to work
in these fucking factories.
Whatever I have to do, I will, I swear.
Would she want me to turn into them?
Would she fold the paper towels closed?
Could I hold her any tighter?
Hello, out there. Hello? Is anybody listening?

after "I have been losing roads" *in* Land to Light On

1.

Truth is: I never found her.
But what's the point of looking now?

Neither woman—my wife, my mute—
understands the sea. How could they?

Down there, she could lift a drawbridge.
She re-arranged the elements.

All those nights on deck,
the polestar pointed nowhere.

If there's only life below,
none of the heavens matter.

2.

The best nights were on my special pillow, outside
his door, the one they use for mastiffs, now.

But, back then, it was odour-free,
hairless, and soft enough.

Better, at least, than my razor-blade follow, better
than the flesh-eating ballets I'd tried.

Would it matter if I could have spoken? Could I have
taken down that asshole diva who took my place?

I see them, sometimes, doing it deep
into each evening, his head fuzzed with heat.

Each kid, remember, has to do what's right;
giving in will cost us centuries.

Should I have put the knife into his lungs, instead?
Is the sea also a garden, really?

Is every human heaven
just another coral fan?

after "The Little Mermaid"

APPLE SUITE

Sweet one, you say, the Ishtar
Gate is just another shoreline,
the closed curtains of a hotel
tryst, its ivory trim, purpled
thighs, angry ceiling spiders.
Our sheets are still damp.

Will we remember your marbled
eye, your blouse, sunlit, on the tiles?
Will we promise sequels?
Will we pretend we didn't know?

There aren't enough bees for the roses,
so pollen covers every pistil.
The tide signals full moon, blood;
its waves could flatten any mansion.
But your dress is no white shell.
Let's let that hilltop boulder roll back down
to where our tangled legs make perfume.
The fish washed up on this beachhead,
the roadkill just over this crest.
Nobody sees us weeping, nobody
offers both cheeks for beating.

If this fruit's a sibling ovary,
are all the cherry blossoms
atom bombs?

I still want this eight-island frog match,
you say, want proper, single words,
want light. But there's more
than one colour, here. My body
is the page, too. My body is seeded.
So if I tell you that *I am trying*

to write a poem, can we still
turn these questions into
new Babylonian blues?

after Naked Poems

Don't ask me about the doll.
I managed that, at least.
And it worked. It doesn't matter how.

That bastard, your father—he was
always looking elsewhere, even
as I rotted, deathside, blanched.

And it cost me. I was stuck
in the graveyard, like Lincoln's kid.
Each cabbage leaf was a desert.

And that Baba Yaga's no trifle, either.
You were right to pocket me,
to follow the breadcrumbs.

Those two horsemen, white and red,
were only minor courtiers.
The black one meant business.

And sure, her mortar might look funny,
but those *human hands for bolts*,
sharp teeth in place of a lock

meant dormant candelabras
and sorted seeds were the only cure
for your sisters' snuffed wicks.

Thank you, Vasilisushka, for the crusted
bread, for your spindly pork, your thin soup.
The meals you offered were skull light.

If you know too much, she said,
you will soon grow old. Remember
that? Were you listening?

When the skull's eyes zapped
your stepfamily, did you blame
me for their ashes?

That I built the loom means nothing,
after all. Each of us spins only
what we're capable of.

He took her by her white hands,
I've read, *seated her by his side,*
and the wedding was celebrated at once.

At once, Vasilisa? All this for a dozen
snug shirts? For another cloistered
version of housebound candles?

And did we really have to
bring your goddamned father
here, too, in the end?

I hope you can still hear me through
these blinkered, emerald walls. I hope you'll
still feed me your new tsar's last bread heels.

after "Vasilisa the Beautiful"

WHAT THEY SAY

They say you're always doing it,
or at least once a decade. Looping

that neo-Nazi meme, where
he gets punched out on the sidewalk,

but with added, 4-D cheekbone crunch,
his blood on our fists.

Why are you still talking rot, then, filth?
Why the same old celebrity wars?

All this downward-dog energy
is no good for you.

Why not just smile? Why not stay put
and purr like a good kitty cat?

We made the locals look
at Buchenwald, they remind you.

Those fuckers shuffling past
the loaded wagons, choking on it.

But you're still just skin and bone.
Why don't you eat something?

Mary Lennox turns out right
in the end, right?

Not every joint's stuffed
with fentanyl.

So why make your cuts
so damned dramatic?

Can't you just try
a little bit harder?

We don't need
to see you like this.

We've got the same pictures of
Auschwitz hair and shoes.

And are we crying about it now?
No, sir!

So why keep on burning
that bra?

Why not just look
on the bright side?

Chew your food before
you swallow.

Always let the receptionist
know you're coming.

after "Lady Lazarus"

BLUEBEARD'S LAST WILL

I.

i.

Whoever would take him
would have him, they're told,
despite his hipster beard.

But that chin is just too much, at first;
his jewel-encrusted country charm falls flat.
It takes an eight-day debauch, all that wine,

for the youngest sister to marry up. Her mom cheers.
And his business trip, a month later, is first-class:
six weeks securing crown land, overseas.

Have fun, he says, leaving.
Invite your friends, even. Feel
free. Here's my key ring.

But, that one little room?
If you go in there, *nothing*
will spare you. Rules are rules.

ii.

Everyone shows up.
They paw the tapestries.
They praise her good-luck rubies.

So, *Fuck him,* she thinks. Her friends
left gaping at diamonds, she almost
breaks her neck on the staircase down.

In the room: the floor *covered with clotted blood.*
In the blood: *the corpses of all the women*
he's married and cut to pieces.

The key falls, of course, and
its bloodstains build another Eve.
He returns before dawn like Jesus might,

all implicit exclamation marks.
You must die, madame, he says,
And you must die quickly.

iii.

Outside, the sun starts shining; the grass
stays green. She prays, shaking,
her smart sister in the tower, hoping for men.

Think of your maker, he says, lifting the sword.
And *What the fuck?* is all she's thinking.
What the fuck?!

Dragoon and musketeer, her brothers
bust in to chop that beard in two;
she inherits everything.

And the moral? *Curiosity costs*, our narrator scolds,
shaking his huge, French wig. And wives
these days? *Good grief*, he moans. *Good God.*

2.

I know what I am
and that's never desperate.

The trips I planned were stations
of the way, first gardens.

But every garden
has its apples.

I believed that. And I believed in her, too.
I honestly thought she'd kill the snake.

Her parties meant nothing, then;
I expected them.

When I went to church, leaving her,
the pews were another country.

I prayed for her strength, not mine.
I thought about that other garden.

And I wanted her to *die quickly*.
That's true.

But I also wanted to stay the axe,
to hold her, to lie down right there.

And I heard them, her brothers,
their horses.

Did I delay on purpose?
Does that make me hellbound?

When they cleaved me in two, after all,
it was her that I pictured, not heaven:

our wedding bed, her shoulders,
the cups of tea she brought me there.

What happens when we hold on
to all the wrong angels?

after "Bluebeard"

49

3

EACH HALF

Those weeds were so long and so thick that no amount of shale
could knock them loose, I thought.

They reached up through their watery V, ready to drift into the
trough I'd blocked with mud, ready to dip my arm into that
silver—that *cold, fucking cold* water, I thought, a bit reckless, not yet
ten—that subarctic creek running straight to our backyard cistern.

I threw so many rocks, my forearms were blurred brackets, a
prime-time Dave Stieb highlight reel, aiming so hard I didn't even
see the break, the one stone sharp enough to click loose the root.

A stalk rose up, and its slowness was a body. It spread out and lay
down. Right there—stone in hand, the violin-string breezes and
all that romance, facing the epicentre of the water my great-great-
grandfather might also have stood beside, deciding to steal into
this minor valley, to build a farm here, to force his own roots into
tough, predictable ground—I understood that the spring was so
deep you could've stuck a whole pickup truck right under, fender
to fender, so this stream might emerge in a gasoline rainbow.

I'd murdered the spring weed. Its leaves were a kid's grey corpse.
It dammed up the water so tight that the pitch of the woods went
baritone.

I dropped my stone and backed into long grass, backed through
an empty field whose insects rubbed against my legs, the narrow
trees slinking into shadows.

I kept in sight the spring, the grey branches, my hometown map
turned to pine bark. Weed in the well. Caution tape. Current.

A PHOTO OF YOU AT ELEVEN

These pre-apocalyptic wedding photos
were printed on real paper,
with actual silver salts,

we'll say, muslin dress buttons
hand-picked in those old Qiaotou
factories; remember?

The barn boards were sanded
to a rusty sheen,
our pictures as keen

as the clean, tin-roof rain,
or wildflowers still filling
the back acreage.

Cowboys in quaint vests, women two-
stepping leather, each ceremony
a new leaf in a family Bible.

In our albums, we're wholesome.
The children we hold, nearly asleep,
nestle right into us.

Outside, the subsoil's roots stay tender;
our underground rivers have not yet dried;
shady oaks guard the lost laneway.

This photo of you, at eleven,
then. Today's the day
we took the picture.

Look.

When the fields crusted over, we skated down the roads.
Everything you've heard is true.

How our parents' storms were so thick they swallowed the
sidewalks, so you traced your route with whatever wires were still
attached to poles, they said. The same wires brought down twenty
years later, iced, millennial.

Or how my grandfather pictured winter horses, their cloudy
exhales; how he strolled each summer concession half a day into
town to buy bread.

How, just kids, we crossed the frozen cash-crop fields on foot,
shovelled the quarry, used our boots for goalposts. Pale little fish
would be trapped down there under the ice, beneath our blades,
clear, and waving weeds would cheer our forward rushes, wind
eclipsing us, our stories already quaint, shadowing worn barstools,
cropping every play.

So maybe the church hill is still a huge rise, and its bells still
bring us home by seven. Maybe, at the park, before the saints
come marching, my red banana-seat bike will lift us over a ridge
of pine trees and become Apollo, that loft and reach, that zero-G
moment before re-entry twists loose handlebars and elbow joints,
before the line drive cracks your forehead in two again, cement set
beneath the Sunday School carpet.

Please don't tell me it must be summer somewhere, a sunray for
sale for centuries now.

Let's inspect our snowflakes, instead. Let's watch these gorgeous
icicles.

Here, hollow; hi there. Here come the thrumming tunnels of the
drainage ditch. If the world's your oyster, its shell must be the rest.

STRAWBERRY ASHBERY

This sunlight through these strawberries
is already only remembered.

They were brought here, the berries, passive,
to this sunlit beach, cooled
by blue frozen packets pulled
from the refrigerator freezer
before we left, bent into the car,
ignited the fuel under controlled,
metallic junctions to pull ourselves
across the map.

When we arrived, cloud cover bruised the lake.
It seems important to remember that light,
especially now, as I eat this berry,
which still holds the electric coolness
carried here by those purposeful machines.

In the water, kids collapse or fight.
On the land, gulls hunt for hot dog buns.
A military plane, a breeze,
someone's beautiful bare back, edged in sand.

All horizons are illusions, I've read,
so up beyond the August sky
every sunray stays radioactive;
our umbrella harnesses just enough
shade for *Self-Portrait in a Convex Mirror.*

I have no berries for you, seagull.

Only these engines, this ink, made,
like the ignited car fuel,
from ancient algae and pressed

plants pulled from the earth
eons later by even more machines
I'd never be able to build, myself.

The light in the berry is refrigerator light.
The light in the lake wants to be the sea.

At age eight at eight feet, I could slice in two a leopard frog's
skull with one well-selected stone. Our country road culverts
were hunting grounds; and all of us were story trolls.

Some lit firecrackers in the mouths of garter snakes. Some hurled
painted turtles into pitch. We crushed the perfect shells of crickets,
the bronze legs of bathroom spiders. We flattened beetles and
fighter-jet damselflies. Spine-wrecked meadow voles, sun-magnified
red ants: we smothered each jewelled body according to custom,
according to charts with Adam on their summits.

Unless our dads were hunters, there were nearly no mammals, just
chipping sparrows felled by gifted BB guns, their graves dug only
later, against the rules, secretly streaked in pine tar. What might
be the measure of what we've killed, then?

Is it this wood mouse, haunted by last night's house cat, its eye
clouded by casual claws, its body captured in Tupperware, then
released, limping, into the driveway? Is it the centipede I found in
our basement then freed into uncut, daylit grass?

None of our libraries have ever held the present. We can't rebuild
a blue mud wasp's thorax.

Our dutiful bird feeders won't answer for the bugs we've flushed
into sewage, the crayfish scooped from the creek, then left to
drown in that well-intended, airless pickle jar.

As kids, maybe it was all white noise and theory. But the worm on
the hook doesn't change.

Each new cast carries its own lost quarry.

GRACELAND T-TUBE

On your floor, morning-shift nurses
suction the gunk from your neck
with sterile tubes, their friendly,
terrible masks telling us that all
the building's medieval scalpels
and ransacked lungs are angelic.
And they are. You'll walk today,
and switch from IV to oral mush.

You'll breathe in, then out again,
and that breathing will reach me, here,
en route, where Festuca grass and still
visible heavenly bodies, god help me,
define as possible the obscene miracles
of blood, of Christmas hymn accidentals.

In the stepdown ICU, the man whose ribs
were cracked open "like a clamshell"
wheezes and double-clicks his morphine.
Ten floors below, the park displays
its sub-zero, crushed-stone modernity;
sunlight holds the tower you see
from your window, moonlight
done and set and gone.

It's still true: our loads and roads
are *shining like a National guitar*.
And I'm moving *down*
the highway, through the cradle
of a sort of *Civil War*.

Beside this two-lane country road,
a red-tailed hawk alights from his live wire
to shadow lustrous, unsuspecting field mice.
We all will be received, he says.

Here's the bridge.

Kids steal stubs and test filters, ignoring each granddad on the
peeling bleachers, the fenced bullpen whirring with warm-up
visitors.

Out on the infield, I scratch a circle with this staked string,
remove the rubber pitcher's slab to hammer it in again at the
right distance for older kids, for men, for the ladies' league, for
measuring tape.

I fill each minor trench with white chalk from a lime bucket,
wobbly wheels and wooden box set against the traced plate.
There are stained-glass angels across the road.

My willy-nilly chalk swerves all the way to the left-field fence,
where home runs get lost in cornstalks, my crooked lines, out
there, eyeballed maybe once an inning. Anywhere a fly lands
might be fair.

The sun sinks over crazy Bristol's house, the north dump blue
and secret, our backyard wells still full. The striped sky makes our
mothers weep, we say. Our fathers, too, but only in the dark.

I lock up the cart, stakes, and strings, replace the batter's box on
its hook, then push up a few rusted switches. The field floods with
yellow, our summer barns vanishing out there: five bucks a diamond.

AUGUST

If a poem could be a tree, it would.
Instead, the traffic sounds like surf
and the leaves are leaves and nothing else.

I've decided. Enough clever sugar.
Enough when-it-really-matters.
Enough hundred-and-ten-percent.

Outside, sheet lightning hugs the cedars.
The far street lamp buries its power lines.
The blue screens hum beneath our thumbs.

Under my fingernails are tiny splinters
from the rosemary stalks picked clean
for tonight's dinner meatballs.

Everyone's gone to bed.
You can hear them groaning into dreams.
The cat has disappeared down a distant hallway.

In yesterday's dream, I'm sure
it all begins with wind and rush
to chart some seaside wingbeat.

But there's rain in the downspout, now.
I hear it. Clouds cancel out the moon.
The picture window's looking in at us.

Beside us, the garbage incinerator converts our plastics to poison clouds. But here, on the inside, forklifts sprint off laden with fresh boxes. Trucks back into lonely orders. The sun is blocked. No one has the right safety shoes.

Our custodian's quitting again, and the crew chief fills the lunchroom—a loft overlooking the floor—with the long-legged narratives of last night's VHS porn flicks.

Back on the clock, machines conceived four decades ago repeat their cautious couplings. The new guy's pinned beneath the new robotics, and our old mechanic rushes from broken interface to busted mould, the foreman leading with little *fuck-yous* and timed blueprints.

Then, break.

Sunset fingers the metal frames around an empty bay, where two men unpack their tiffins: sandwiches and sad granola bars. Their brothers, over there, are fixing iron rifle sights on one another's kids.

Here, they keep quiet, then toast the factory floor, their punch cards.

The loading bays are mostly empty. The exit signs are mostly red.

KEEPING FIRE

> To turn, and remember, that
> is the fruit.
> —John Thompson

I.

Childhood atlases in adult cellars,
pirate- or space-ships grounded in garages,
our boots crunch gravel.

We're walking midnight-hour railroad tracks,
each star resting on a crown of maples,
houses awash in blue-TV sunsets.

A coal seam or gold strike
could be here, below us,
awaiting spades,

but our tired hip sockets need children,
fresh and keen from running
winter wheat fields.

Some of our jeans carry burrs from those meadows,
burrs like grandparents plucking clean
pianos, pancakes, plush.

In some: metric expansion,
cosmic inflation, or
the whip of water to earth.

This daughter's refugee-tent lullaby.
This woman with new bruises for a yawning cop.
This man making couch-cushion forts.

The coals are still warm.

2.

Steam engines can't turn;
they follow just one feeling.
Their stokers tell us every fire needs a shovel.

Some are like those elements
that begin bleeding energy
the moment they're plucked from bedrock.

How can we hold them close?

We walk the midnight rails to sunrise,
our steps echoing forest or prairie,
the sea a distant dream, the sky alive with planets.

If there's snow, it doubles the moonlight
to the end of the line, where we'll drift
into a station house for coffee

and click on a gas furnace,
its blue heat encircling our bodies.
Here's the keeping fire, then.

We walk from station to station
lit by unseen orbits.
The sun will come back, we say.

And mean it.

KANGHWA HAIBUN

I have always thought that the miracle of birds is not that they fly, but that they touch down.
—Helen Humphreys

Four hundred feet in the seaward air, we walked this island's thin avenue, folded against shore. We've lost that sense of wind, now.

But we know the island's name, its next-door airport. We landed there—remember?—in another life. Just north, just east, are the hidden missile installations we've since read about back home. But there are also temples and chili peppers spread on blankets, readying for winter kimchi pots. There are rice fields like stained-glass uniforms, expertly arranged around darkness.

Up there, we believed in the old west wind. We walked a fine dirt path, perhaps three feet wide, and found relief. The relief was a giant cliffside Buddha. It was facing cumulus clouds that were out over the water. It might have been a month or a millennium old, the Buddha. It might have been the answer we wanted to build. It might have been that old *dream of a common language*.

We swung our arms to signal youth, aimed our film cameras at the rock's robes. We focused and clicked. We watched and listened. We thought about the postcards we'd mail to Ontario relatives, but we only thought so far. The path was too narrow not to pay attention to; the treed drop was gorgeously sheer. The bamboo apex was where every language stopped. The clay pots back in the city were set against this salted wind. The stone relief looked right past us.

Years later, the chisel that made this is still working. We can hear it. And we're still climbing. We've sweated through our undershirts. Step. Trail. Buddha. Mouth. Bamboo. Breeze. Relief.

Worn gravel, tethered updraft, prints. There are birds, here. None of them alight.

4

JUST LINE

LINEUP

1. Super—

This is no green-screen canyon.
It's real-life fire, real-time fighting;
each rib counts, we think, all our biceps.

If we hold your spandex contrail,
a sample on the plate,
we find, there, every missile.

Remember: he's only at home, really,
surrounded by skyscraper ice crystals.
Is every one a mirror?

2. *Boogey—*

Those nails chipped
on the dirt-packed floor
are already set,

called on to hook
another body
in Bluebeard's closet.

We use his hairy fists to make gentle
our raging lullabies or dulcet diapers,
to aim Bibles into playpens,

to return
to the basement,
ready for sacrament.

The answer to any
specific box
is just another lid.

3. *The Last—*

We've not only met him,
but been him: beachfront,
tattered, wrecked.

He eats urchins or monkeys
or squirrels, tasered
with jam and dirt.

So he's gross, that's true.
But from bamboo he can also
build cities or glass or circuitry.

When the WiFi's dead
again,
he taps a new aquifer.

Frankenstein's a failure, he thinks,
his kid left on that ice floe, stupid ass.
I'm the prime minister of possible.

Any rope thrown
over the lowest limb
will yield the simplest apples.

4. *The First*—

Was following instructions.
He named the best he could,
I guess.

And he named his enemy, too:
snake, tree, mirror,
ivy, woman.

5.—kind

If that old chestnut on the ground
isn't artificial, we'll fill
our cedar chests with luck.

All glorious, all-time,
all the lotus-eaters
in Herodotus,

we parade each new
algorithmic certainty
to sell our golden oldies.

The sky these days
as blue as ever, the same
set plumb lines left unread.

When this wave pulls
your feet down into the sand,
we're all at the mercy of bigger things.

6.—*made*

The pages are white,
still. Their borders
set to default.

We insist on, then rip off
make-up. You'll do,
you say, what you like.

The Goldilocks Zone,
you say, is where the past
and present fuse.

If you can't see
your own shackles,
they'll rattle the windows closed.

I HOLD THE DOOR

It is best to pin insects soon after they die and while they are still relaxed to minimize breaking any body parts.

If this is not possible, you can soften insects in a relaxing jar.

—Jeffrey Hahn, University of Minnesota

We're doing this, trained
that elbows on the table are rude,
that talking with your mouth
full signals redneck rust.

In the snowbanks, litter
collects in glimmering reds.
Car exhaust fuzzes the afternoon sun.
All classes will continue despite the weather.

What can you say, invited
through this frame, wooden
studs inside the walls
holding the room's right angles?

If neckties come next,
will we hold the doors for them?

This is no place for apology.
The words we use are action figures.
Let's admit our polite elbows
are nothing less than locked.

The men who fill the village square
shout down public bodies.
Their speeches swell into fists.
It's not about revolving glass.

It's about the women's heads,
bent, as though in prayer,
as they pass our open fingers.
This is no grace note.

We've already pinned each specimen
to heavenly white stock.

Here, in my body,
are doors and hammers.

We pitch cooler tallboys
across lockdown dress sweat,

set each frame
with our fathers' tools.

Here, in my starched shirt
the keys release the pins,

the hedges trimmed
just so;

access and access and access
and still we mourn absolutes,

still we label excess as danger,
still we "man" the roadblocks.

At our workstations, we update
our chemistry sets with enriched uranium.

We've begun a list of who
should reach the launch pads.

Here, with my diamond bracelet,
we match good wine with rare cuts.

There's only the singular, we think.
There's only the highway.

There's still these same old borders
on our colour-tinted treasure maps.

It gets in the lungs, less corona than corolla. It roots there.
Maybe a birth defect, true. Maybe complications due
to the fixed-focus lighting of certain obstetric suites.
Maybe this is how it gets in the trachea, collecting there.

Asymptomatic until disturbed, then pollination.
Asymptomatic until external stimuli trigger
organic chain reactions, trigger blood cell
production, hormonal release, insulin distribution.

Ingestion of processed carbohydrates and refined sugars
clearly linked to cell mutation, division, replication.
Ingestion of certain nitrates clearly linked to the lungs,
to swollen linings, autoimmune response.

It gets in the lungs, whether dormant at birth or exacerbated by diet.
It clings to the bronchi, weighting them like divers. It fills
the trachea with mucous, the alveoli where the bronchioles
terminate: heavy grapes at late harvest, perfectly suited for ice wine.

Here, at the base of the pleurae, above the diaphragm, it gets in the lungs.
See, here, not only comparative indexes of plant, animal, vegetable.
See, here, also various ships still engaged in crossings. See, here, homemade
militia stockpiles, the crossbow this pharmacist keeps in his basement,

just in case, he says. Just in case. See, here, where the lungs'
cells metastasize, still, on the outside, asymptomatic. Until
hiccups, then coughs, then fever. Until the previously clear
oxygen of each intake turns cloudy, narrowed, forced.

Confirmation: it's airborne. It's in the lungs. Confirmation:
everyone, as on *The Walking Dead*, is already infected. Everyone
transforms given the proper stimuli. Everyone eventually
requires a sleek blade, a shattering bullet, a careful arrow.

I am sitting here at my desk, breathing. My diaphragm, beneath
my pleurae, internalized against the lungs, asymptomatic. The crop-dusters
from my father's youth also meant no harm. They spread promise
across their fields. Their noxious clouds made every sunset sparkle.

So I am sitting here, asymptomatic, getting in the lungs. Framed
on my blue walls are pictures of giant sequoias and Douglas firs
and pristine beaches. Squared on my neat shelves are outdated
guidebooks and antique maps, collected and arranged for easy access.

I've gotten, in the lungs, such simplified mitosis. I've gotten, in the lungs,
certain photographs of arrival, carried like burrs on my jeans, perhaps,
alongside each invasive old-world spore, every pioneer sermon delivered
against hand-hewn logs, split, settled, set ablaze. We're all infected.

In the lungs, here, asymptomatic, exhaling our fathers' luminous crop dust.

5

EVERY SPAN

THE END OF THE BOAT

If you're unsure of parenthood,
of swells,

if your spirit hooks
wrestle pillow books,

if the trite sunset
painting makes you weep,

if the baby, the dividends,
the slapstick funeral parlour,

if the epigraph's
a misquote,

if the charity infomercial starring
Baptist American celebrities,

if the powerful autumn is shelved,
then opened, then shelved, then Shelley,

if the marriage, the adultery,
the Google translations,

then, *the seaweed in his hair*
the fish had eaten his testicles

the gulls had pecked out his eyes
the brass chains on his wrists.

19/85

1.

Dear friends, have I given you October?
How the deepest lakes fill with blue?
Or the tired hills turn to vinyl sleeves?
You've seen it before, I know.

But still. It's here.

2.

They've cut the earth for you
into tight, crisp cubes.
Chestnut horses by the pond, that breeze.
From here, you can still see

where the old ports met
their muddy banks, cleaved
Ecclesiastes into bread.
Some of that was yours. Remember?

3.

I've chosen lines for your mother.
The ones with cracks that let the light on in.
They tack them up beside your pictures,
eternally looping on the closed-circuit TV.

There's nothing smart to say.

4.

Out in the field, you already knew that.
We all get basement cake
when the service finally ends,
you said. Why not share the recipe?

5.

Along the highway, they've finally
patched the busted bridge.
It holds my car above a tiny creek
filled with microscopic things
already preparing for winter.

All of us are riding the brake.

FROM HALF A BACKYARD BIRCH

It was less wind or lightning
than willpower, really.

This fungus: I've been growing it for years.
It was me that let the termites in, right here, at this knot.

That my other half still makes oxygen
means we're a classic mask; we're that shore

you've dreamt about, our glory days
tapped into the earth, drinking.

For years I've seen you all bud and bloom
and die off again, buried in winters.

But that night, when the seam split
and my timber let loose,

I watched the earth rise up
and break my spine to pieces.

From here, the house cat in the picture
window just looks ordinary.

Is middle age the same
as the middle of the river?

When my late April robins relocate to aluminum
downspouts, pileated woodpeckers to fresh decay,

I'm okay with that. Settle in
for the season, I tell myself.

Here, years later, the yard spring-damp,
you'll find what's left of me:

a black-sheep softened hull, a riot of peeling bark,
the last leaves, just so, every petal green.

ESTUARY

Offshore, we search the map
for rivers in the thickened ink.
We're hunting for fracture,
for a fault line we can depend on
to interrupt each shifting plate.
The earth, we've said, is a set-up.
The map, we read, is a signpost.
We're looking for indivisible
latitudes, for absolute bearings.

It's imperative, in this search,
that you don't just trust the way I lead
to summits or valleys or furlough.
It's important, instead, that you check
the manner in which someone has fixed
the ropes and ladders above us,
their tanks already stowed, the ones
we trust, the ones we think are full.
It's imperative not that you just believe

what I'm telling you, but that you think
belief is possible, that across the map
may be jungle or clearing or settlement
or war. I wanted to believe, I might
tell you, that those searching
for fracture believed in fair-trade
chocolate, in Coltrane and millennial
handmade stitching. But *terra nullius*
is nobody's national anthem.

I've chosen to believe, instead, in women
who see women, *fully dressed*, stepping from the river;
none of them will fail to check the ropes,
none will push their own slow mothers
into a crevasse. Search for weeds in the lawn
and you'll find them. Search for green
and you'll ignore the poison leaching
into playground swing sets.
You don't have to believe me.

Let's assume, instead, that every map
is already a map of system, that every
jungle is already tracer fire, that each
and every tree contains combustion,
that these spent shells held signal flares
fired from the deck of the boat
that brought me here,
that every word we pick
already knows its capital.

EIGHTEENTH-CENTURY COMET

If we study, say, eighteenth-century
sentimentalism, we might also understand
the Kuiper Belt comet nuclei
these radio voices keep talking about.
Both aim beyond the earth's
own deflection shield.
Don't they wish they could move
past theory? Don't they want a pet
rock returned intact from
their chosen outer spaces?

The owner of this coffee shop
passed away this winter.
Her picture spills across the window
seat where I've been perched for
centuries if we measure by midday light.

We can't really move back
to the last subway station, can we?
Each tattoo will sag into body failure.
We're all astronomers of this Americano,
scholars of bad dialogue.

The difference, the radio tells me,
between comets and asteroids
is not as clear as it used to be.
Those tails made from melted ices
(they say, in the plural) are not
exclusive in their dust ignition.
It's not just rock.

All the old models are rotting
meat ensnared in cellophane.
The mould on the bread
is a record of longing.

The radio, the coffee cup, the photograph,
the comets, the voices, the sunlight:
old brushstrokes made
on this faux-tin ceiling:
not the chair's seat, but its hand-turned
spindles loaded into the lathe:
not the napkin, but the chainsaw
in the forest, toppers holding giants:
not the first edition or final, drafted page,
but the ink from the well from the long gone
prehistoric plankton pickled underground:

the subject of every study
seems to be the space between us;

the aim of every telescope
is the memory of our finest apple.

THE ENDS OF THE EARTH

I can't imagine saying *Baby*, saying
as a matter of fact, saying
anything on Spain's plain rain.

And, yes; I know they used to call cargo
manifests "middlemen," to fill
the ends of the earth with ink.

Still, I can't imagine more straws
clogging the reef, the spent oxygen
tanks glistening on Everest,

Lhasa's pebbled monasteries or those *men
without skin,* all rich real estate brokers,
money where their mouths should be.

Is every blue box just
another hit and run? Each new
release: a derelict strip mine?

The last time we talked about this,
it might have been 1995, our reckless
late-model sedans airbag-free.

The deer in the back forty were still
local, then; and our grandfathers still plunged
their fingers into the garden and unearthed rain.

So, maybe it matters that I'm putting my wrist,
now, into this very cold country stream.
That I'm pulling out this metamorphic stone

smooth as all our syllables.
Let's imagine how to put
our faith in that.

Last night, after setting a last-minute bag
of trash into the can deposited
already at the curb, I stretched out
on the cracked asphalt of our driveway.
It was dark out, and up there, the same
clouds and stars paraded that always do.

You're talking about them now,
quoting a psychologist
who has been noting that
they're always present, just hidden
behind glaring sunshine.
Can that fact be the one that saves us?

And you're telling me this in writing.
Here, in my hands, is your new book.
I brush the overhead tree's red dust
from the pages, but the red dust
turns out to be some bug,
whose body is now smeared across
this paragraph talking about war
and environmental destruction.

You tell me *There are no big solutions coming.*
This is disappointing and troubling.
But *It may also be a relief.*
Are these things true only in
the country between us?

There are more bugs on the page now
but I've learned not to think
of them as only dust.
The polymer pond before me
gurgles wonderfully so I can barely hear
myself turning your careful pages.

You're in a September heat wave
but I'm thousands of miles
from where you live in California,
surrounded by the sorts of trees drawn
from memory by Dr. Seuss
down at La Jolla Cove,
where I once swam with sea lions
who were prehistoric and lethal
in the water around me.

And now I'm thinking how that red dust blood bug
will always mark the pages where you considered
what could save your country.

I'm thinking of the trash, held like an infant
in the arms of the garbage can,
to be opened in the morning by strangers
and driven off towards mountains
of other similar bags, all bound for burial.

Your father had just died when we met.
And now both of us are fathers,
and this means something essential
when I read about you lofting a football
in 1976 to your brother or lamenting
elections lost or slowly putting together
each rocking horse upon which
our pages are perched
like awkward, shoeless carnival kids.

Can you picture the driveway
and what lying back in the dust made
happen to the eavestroughs and rooftop
and the neighbour's coniferous trees
that always line that view?

Can we ever really hold a body's blueprint,
a trash collector's head line, any early Venus
resting on its bare, galactic blade?

I'd like to think we can.
I'd like to think it doesn't matter
what we meant.

NOTES AND ACKNOWLEDGEMENTS

Some poems have previously appeared (sometimes in different form) in the following:

- "Red Bed" in *Working in the Dark: Homage to John Thompson* (Anchorage Press, 2014)
- "Keeping Fire" in *The Fiddlehead*
- "Speed Trap" and "The End of the Boat" in *The Malahat Review*
- "All The Wind Turbines" in *The Puritan*
- "19/85" on *Dusie*
- "Escarpment" in *Arc Poetry Magazine*
- "A Dozen Morning Translations" in *Vallum Magazine*

Hearty thanks to every editor.

—

"Thank God You're Normal" is constructed with actual historic predictions of the future; its title is what our new neighbour said to me when our family moved in beside them.

Speeds noted in "The Great Attractor" were borrowed from Rhett Herman's 1998 *Scientific American* article "How fast is the earth moving?"

Part 2 comprises loose English-to-English translations of the following: "The Frog King, or Iron Heinrich" (1819) by Jacob and Wilhelm Grimm (trans. Ralph Manheim); "Trying to Talk with a Man" in *Diving into the Wreck* (1973) by Adrienne Rich; "The Story of Grandmother" (1885) by Paul Delarue (trans. Austin E. Fife); "I have been losing roads" in *Land to Light On* (1997) by Dionne Brand; "The Little Mermaid" (1843) by Hans Christian Andersen (trans. Erik Haugaard); *Naked Poems* (1965) by Phyllis Webb; "Vasilisa the Beautiful" (1855) by Aleksandr Afanas'ev (trans. Norbert Guterman); "Lady Lazarus" in *Ariel* (1965) by Sylvia Plath;

97

and "Bluebeard" (1697) by Charles Perrault (trans. Angela Carter). The English-language source for each fairy tale is the fifth edition of Broadview's *Folk and Fairy Tales* anthology, edited by Martin Hallett and Barbara Karasek; a few short phrases borrowed from this volume appear in italics in the poems. A line in "Bluebeard's Last Will" alters the title of Phyllis Webb's collection *The Sea Is Also A Garden* (1962).

"Graceland T-Tube" concerns my partner's recovery from a sub-glottic tracheal re-section; huge thanks to Dr. Andrew Pierre, Dr. Salvatore Privitera (at Southlake), and the miraculous nurses at Toronto General Hospital.

Quoted or closely referenced lines and titles appear in italics through-out (though not all italics are quotations and not all references are italicized), including the following: "But We Don't Live In A Per-fect World": "In Those Years" in *Dark Fields of the Republic* (1995) by Adrienne Rich; "Red Bed": *Thompson & Morgan*'s seed catalogue entry for "Chipman's Canada Red"; "Escarpment": *An Atlas of the Difficult World* (1991) by Adrienne Rich and "Postscript" in *The Spirit Level* (1996) by Seamus Heaney; "A Social History Of Tone Deafness": "Trying to Talk with a Man" in *Diving into the Wreck* (1973) by Adrienne Rich; "Apple Suite": *Naked Poems* (1965) by Phyllis Webb; "Graceland T-Tube": Paul Simon's song "Graceland" on *Graceland* (1986); "Keeping Fire": *Stilt Jack* (1978) by John Thompson; "Kanghwa Haibun": *The Evening Chorus* (2016) by Helen Humphreys and *The Dream of a Common Language* (1978) by Adrienne Rich; "I Hold the Door": "Collecting and preserving insects" by Jeffrey Hahn on the University of Minnesota Extension website; "The End of the Boat": "The Boat" (1968) by Alistair MacLeod in *Island* (2000) and *The Lost Salt Gift of Blood* (1976); "Estuary": Toni Morrison interviewed in *Toni Morrison: The Pieces I Am* (2019) directed by Timothy Greenfield-Sanders; "The Ends of the Earth": *Beloved* (1987) by Toni Morrison; "What We Meant": *Why Poetry* (2017) by Matthew Zapruder and *The Country Between Us* (1981) by Carolyn Forché.

—

Huge thanks to Anita Lahey and Sachiko Murakami, who offered invaluable comments on many of these poems.

Grateful cheers, too, to Gil Adamson, David O'Meara, Erin Wunker, and Matthew Zapruder for their generous close readings.

Enormous thanks, also, to the behind-the-scenes superstars at M&S, especially Kelly Joseph, Emma Dolan, and Peter Norman.

Finally, for her superlative clarity, courage, and friendship, both on-screen and off-, I'm so grateful to my editor, Dionne Brand. Thank you, Dionne, for all the maps you've made for me.

—

"Red Bed" is for John Thompson's rhubarb patch, with kudos to Thaddeus Holownia.

"A Photo Of You At Eleven" is for Davis.

"19/85" is for Alicia Clark (1997-2017) and Eldon Hay (1931-2017).

"What We Meant" is for Matthew Zapruder.

"Graceland T-Tube" and "Kanghwa Haibun" are for Kristal.

Love and thanks to all.

© Kristal Davis

ROB WINGER is the author of three previous collections of poetry, including *Muybridge's Horse*, a *Globe and Mail* Best Book and CBC Literary Award winner, which was also a finalist for the Governor General's Literary Awards, Trillium Book Award for Poetry, and Ottawa Book Award. He lives in the hills northeast of Toronto, where he teaches at Trent University.